'O marenariello
The Sailor

S. Gambardella

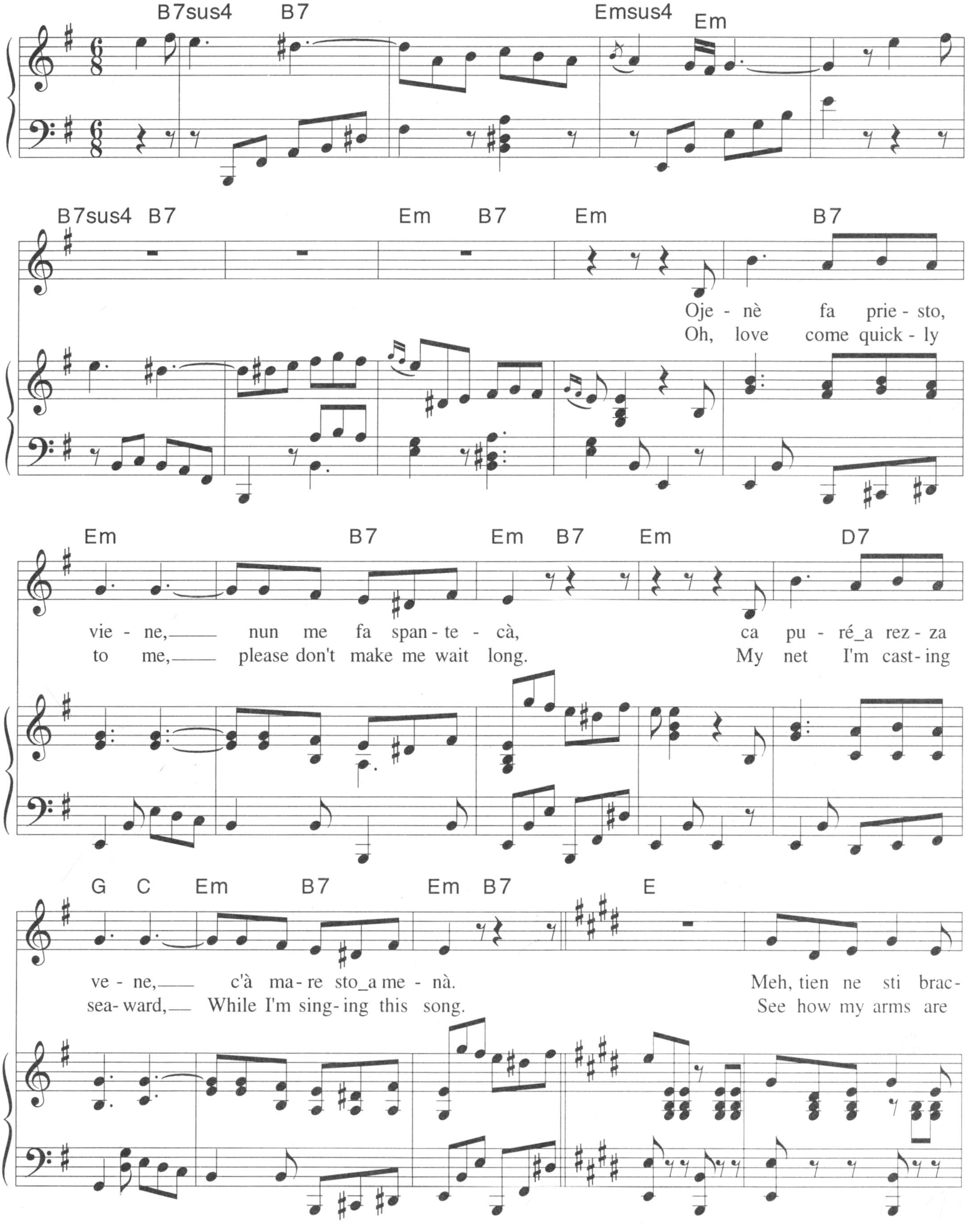
B7sus4 B7 Emsus4 Em
B7sus4 B7 Em B7 Em B7
Oje - nè fa prie - sto,
Oh, love come quick - ly
Em B7 Em B7 Em D7
vie - ne, nun me fa span - te - cà, ca pu - ré_a rez - za
to me, please don't make me wait long. My net I'm cast - ing
G C Em B7 Em B7 E
ve - ne, c'à ma - re sto_a me - nà. Meh, tien ne sti brac -
sea - ward, While I'm sing - ing this song. See how my arms are

Mel Bay Presents
ITALIAN SONGS & ARIAS
CANZONI E ARIE ITALIANE

By Jerry Silverman

INTRODUZIONE

This collection celebrates the joy of singing. It contains a potpourri of vocal gems in Italian and in the Neapolitan dialect. It is dedicated to all lovers of the vocal art, so richly fulfilled by the melodies of *la bella Italia*.

You will encounter herein, a world of sunshine and sorrow, lovers and leavers, seascapes and landscapes, mandolins, guitars and, above all, balconies – beneath which, hearts (breaking and otherwise) pour out their deepest emotions.

Some of the world's greatest composers and singers have expressed themselves in this sublime musical language. Now it is up to you to clear your throat and have a go at it.

Enjoy!

Jerry Silverman

EVANSTON PUBLIC LIBRARY
1703 ORRINGTON AVENUE
EVANSTON, ILLINOIS 60201

© 1996 BY MEL BAY PUBLICATIONS, INC., PACIFIC, MO 63069.
ALL RIGHTS RESERVED. INTERNATIONAL COPYRIGHT SECURED. B.M.I. MADE AND PRINTED IN U.S.A.

Visit us on the Web at http://www.melbay.com — E-mail us at email@melbay.com

Contents

Canzoni/Songs

'O marenariello/The Sailor 3
Lu cardillo/The Goldfinch 6
La Spagnola/The Spanish Girl 8
Il bacio/The Kiss 11
Carnivale di Venezia/Carnival Of Venice 14
Serenata Napolitana/Neapolitan Serenade 16
O sole mio/Oh, My Sunshine 20
Funiculi Funicula 22
Serenata/Serenade 25
Mandolinata/Mandolin Song 28
Torna a Sorrento/Come Back To Sorrento 31
Vieni sul mar/Come To The Sea 34
Io the vurria vasa/I Would Like To Kiss You 36
A Frangesa/The French Girl 39
Addio a Napoli/Farewell To Naples 42
Santa Lucia 44
A serenata de' rose/The Serenade Of The Roses 46
Oje Caruli/Oh, My Caroli' 49
Primavera/Springtime 52
Luna nova/New Moon 54
Mattinata/Morning Serenade 56
Dall'Italia noi siamo partiti/When From Italy We Did Take Our Leave 60
La rondinella dell' emigrato/The Emigrant's Swallow 62
Il Sirio/The Sirio 64

Arie/Arias

Dalla sua pace/On Her Contentment 66
Deh vieni alla finestra/Oh, Come To Your Window 70
Una furtiva lagrima/A Furtive Tear 73
La donna è mobile/Woman Is Changeable 76
La Lola bianca/Oh, Lola, Fairest 80
M'appari tutt' amor/She Seemed To Me 84
Ah sì, ben mio/Ah Yes, My Love 88
Vesti la giubba/Put On The Jacket 92

Lu cardillo
The Goldfinch

Il bacio
The Kiss

Luigi Arditi

Serenata Napolitana
Neapolitan Serenade

P. Mario Costa

O sole mio
Oh, My Sunshine

Eduardo di Capua

Funiculi Funicula

Written to celebrate the opening of the funicular railway on Mt. Vesuvius in 1880

Luigi Denza

Serenata
Serenade

Words by Alfredo Silvestri
Music by Enrico Toselli

Mandolinata
Mandolin Song

Emile Paladilhe

Allegretto con spirito

Sù_an - diam! la notte è bel - la, La luna va spun - tar. Di qua, di là, per la città, Andiam cia tras - tul - lar. Fin chè la notte
Let's go! the night is won - drous, The moon is com - ing out. And here and there and ev - 'ry - where, Let's wan - der through the town. As long as night per -

Io te vurria vasa
I Would Like To Kiss You

Words by Vincenzo Russo
Music by Eduardo di Capua

A Frangesa
The French Girl

P. Mario Costa

Addio a Napoli
Farewell To Naples

Teodoro Cottrau

Santa Lucia

A serenata de' rose
The Serenade Of The Roses

Eduardo di Capua

Oje Caruli
Oh, My Caroli'

P. Mario Costa

Primavera
Springtime

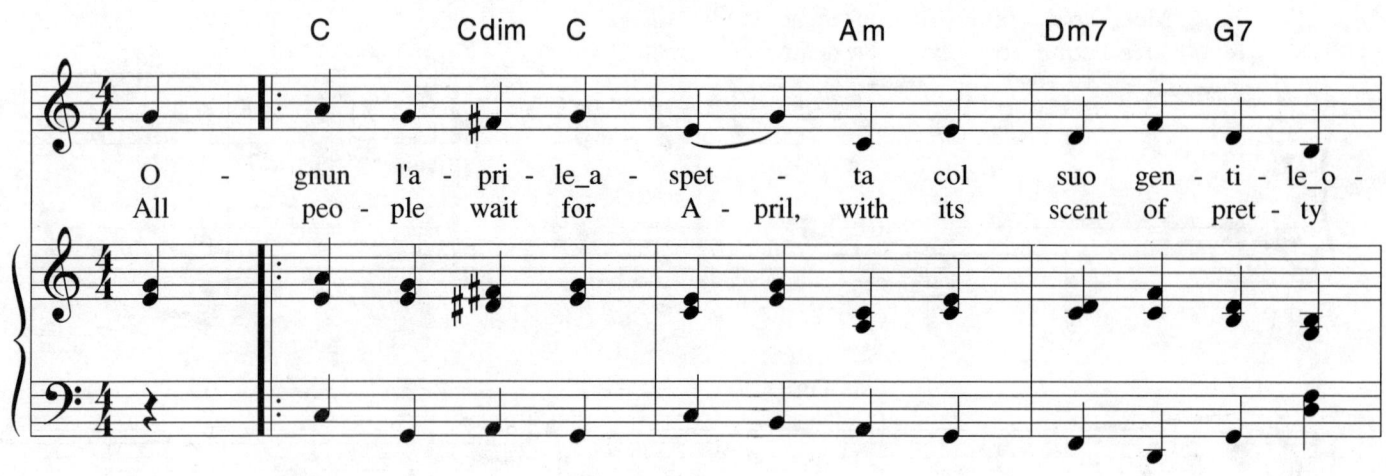
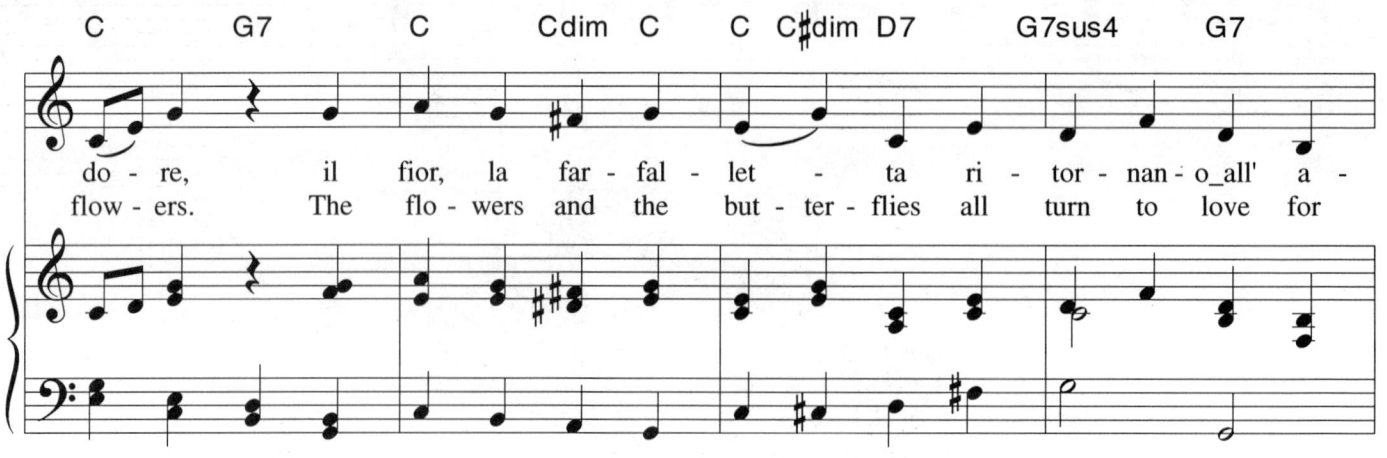

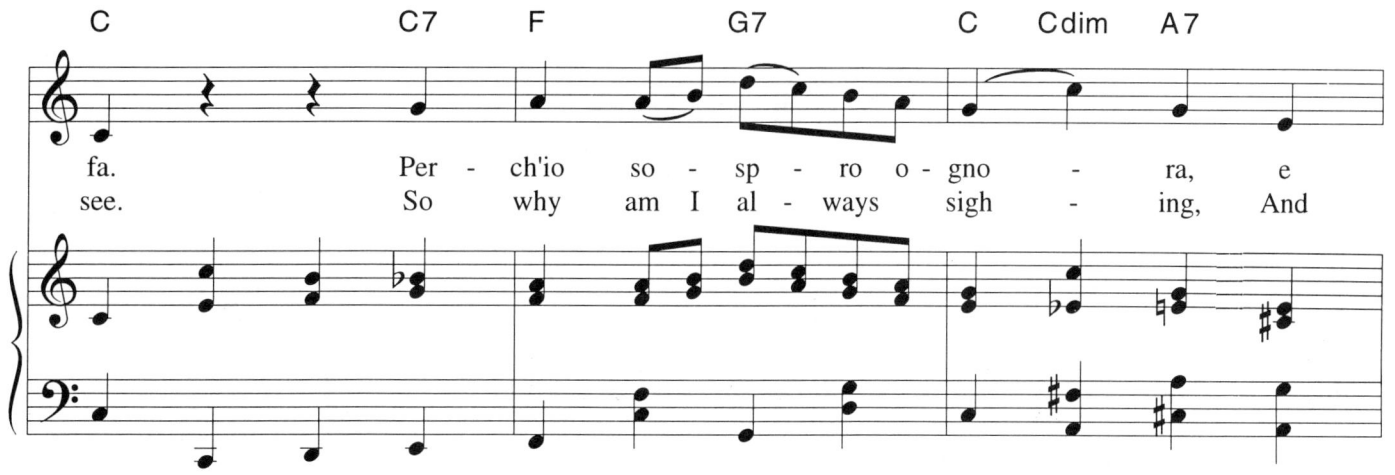

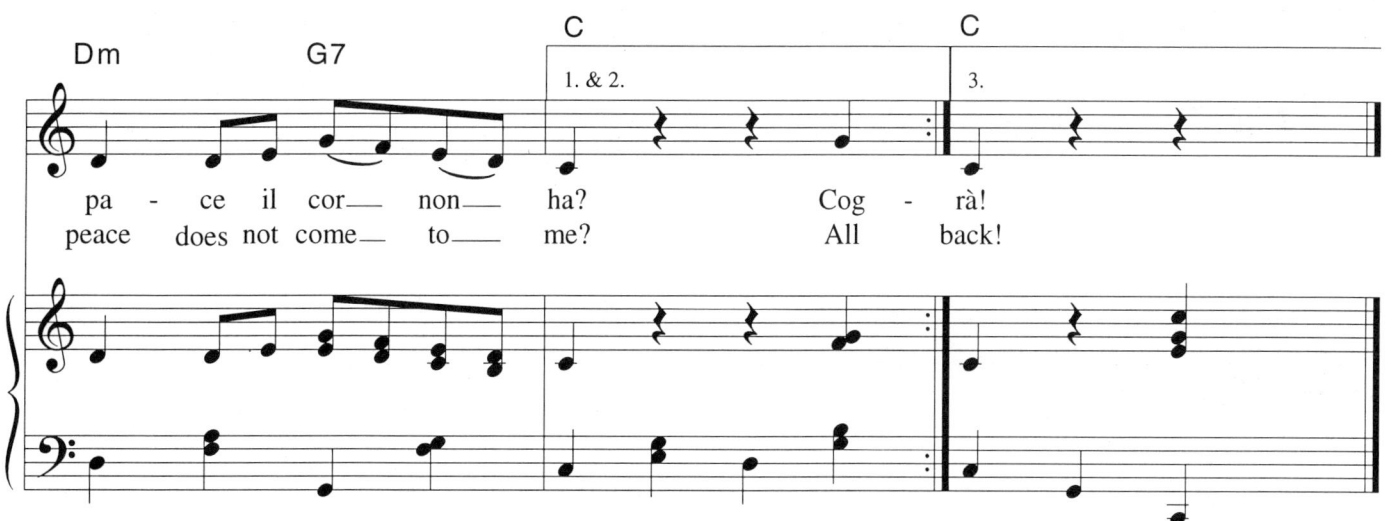

Cogliete, voi, viole,	All out to pick the violets,
Fanciulle, in primavera:	Go young girls in the springtime.
Raggio per me di sole	The sun's rays do not warm me,
Non v'ha che dica: spera.	I'm hoping one will be mine.
Vïole e roselline	The violets and the roses
Il prato ognor vi diè:	Are there for all to see,
Io colgo solo spine,	But only thorns I gather –
Un fior non v'ha per me.	No flowers are for me.
La luna col suo raggio	The moon in all its glory,
Or tutto fa d'argento:	All silver is glowing.
E pur ritorna il maggio,	Soon May will be returning,
E fa ritorno il vento;	Soft winds, they will be blowing.
Ogni stagione viene,	Each season comes 'round duly,
Ogni anno se ne va:	The years just pass, alack!
Chi mi voleva bene	The one that I love truly,
Ahi! più non tornerà!	Will nevermore come back.

Luna nova
New Moon

Valse allegretto　　　　　　　　　　　　　　　　　　　　　　　　**P. Mario Costa**

La lu - na no - va ncopp' a lu ma - re sten - ne na
The new moon shines down o - ver the o - cean, stretched in a

fa - scia d'ar - gien - to fi - no, dint' a la var - ca nu ma - re -
bright line of fin - est sil - ver, Straight to the boat in which a young

na - re qua - se s'ad - dor - me c'á rez - za nzi - no.
sail - or Is al - most sleep - ing, his net on his lap now.

Mattinata
Morning Serenade

Ruggiero Leoncavallo

Dall'Italia noi siamo partiti
When From Italy We Did Take Our Leave

Well, I came to America because I heard the streets were paved with gold. When I got here I found out three things: first, the streets weren't paved with gold; second, they weren't paved at all; and third, I was expected to pave them. (An Italian immigrant's recollections, Ellis Island Museum)

All'America noi siamo arrivati,
Non abbiam trovato né paglia né fieno.
Abbiam dormito sul nudo terreno;
Come le bestie abbiam riposá'. *Chorus*

But when we did arrive in America,
Neither hay nor straw was to be found.
We were forced to sleep upon the ground;
Just like animals we had to rest. *Chorus*

L'America l'è lunga e l'è larga.
L'è formata di monti e di piani.
E con l'industria di noi altri italiani,
Abbiam fondato paesi e cittá. *Chorus*

O, America is long and it is very wide.
It is made up of mountains and broad plains.
With the hard work of all of us Italians,
We have built up the city and the land. *Chorus*

La rondinella dell' emigrato
The Emigrant's Swallow

The music to this *romanza* was impossible to locate. It would have been a pity not to have included it in this collection. Accordingly, I set it to an original melody in the hope that the swallow might once again take wing.

Music by Jerry Silverman

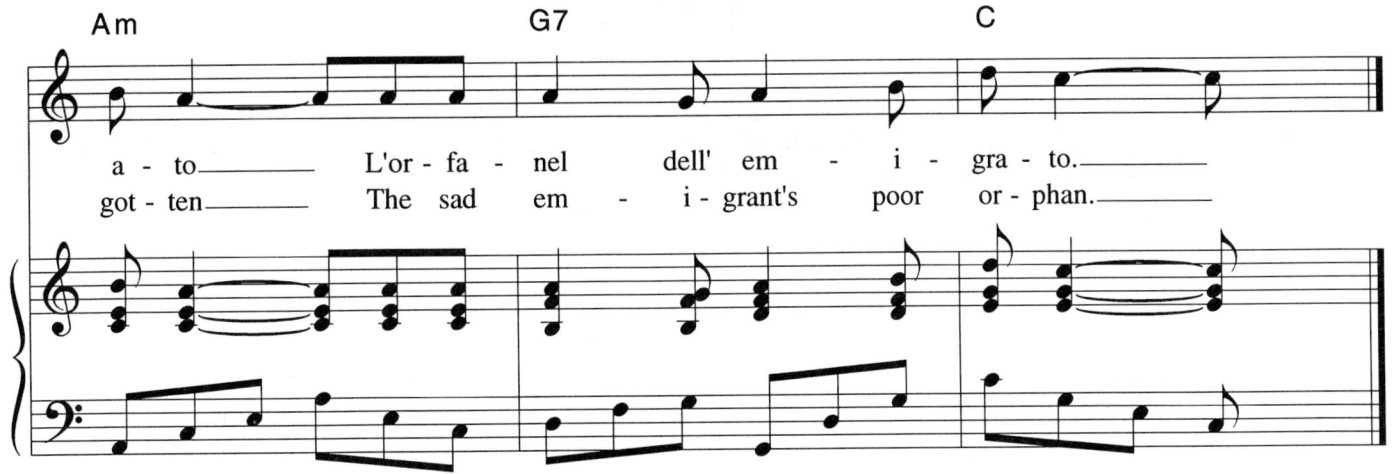

Se dall' alte dell' empiro,	From the heights as you go flying,
Tu ravvisi il tetto mio,	If you see my roof way down there,
E odi il suono d'un sospiro,	And you hear my plaintive sighing,
O una prece alzata a Dio.	As to God I send a faint prayer—
Ferma il volo e ti riposa,	Stop your flight and come to rest,
Sopra il sen della mia sposa.	Pause a while on my wife's breast.
Nella soglia abbandonata	On the balcony so lonely
Forma il nido o Rondinella;	Is your nest, o little swallow;
Sulle penne equilibrata	And your feathers know the journey
Tu del profugo favella.	That a refugee must follow.
E col gemito natiò,	And with your plaintive cry,
Addormenta il figlio mio.	Sing my son a lullaby.
Te beata! almen potrai	Blessed are you beyond measure
Del mio mar veder le spume.	To observe my sea's foam quiver.
Del mio ciel goder i rai,	My sky's sun rays give you pleasure,
Bever l'onda del mio fiume.	And you drink from my own river.
E vagar sera e mattina	Morn' and night you range so wide
Sulla patria, mia collina.	O'er my country's green hillside.
Ti rammenta ch'io t'accolsi,	You remember I did save you,
Traboccata fuor del nido;	When down from your nest you tumbled.
Alla madre non ti tolsi,	To your mother then I gave you,
Che ti chiese con un grido,	While she flew around and grumbled.
Ti rammenta che il mio tetto	Just remember that you nested
Fu tua culla e tuo ricetto.	On my roof—that's where you rested.
Repeat first verse	*Repeat first verse*

Il Sirio
The Sirio

On August 4, 1906, the Italian steamship *Sirio,* out of Genoa, bound for Montevideo and Buenos Aires with 690 passengers, struck a reef near the Horrnigas Islands off Cabo Palos on the Mediterranean coast of Spain. There was a chaotic struggle for the few lifeboats, and 422 people drowned.

Sull' alto mare la nave s'infranse,
Incontrando lo scoglio fatale.
Quattro barchette scorrevan sull'acque
In soccorso dei nostri fratelli. *Chorus*

Tra quei naufraghi i Preti pregavano,
E poi lor davano la benedizione.
Padri e madri baciavano i figli,
Poi sparivano tra le onde del mare. *Chorus*

While on the high sea, the *Sirio* shattered
When it ran against the reef of misfortune.
Four little lifeboats sped over the water,
Hoping to rescue our brothers that day. *Chorus*

Among these shipwrecked ones the priests prayed to heaven,
And they gave them their last benediction.
Fathers and mothers, they kissed their dear children,
And then they sank beneath the waves of the sea. *Chorus*

Deh vieni alla finestra
Oh, Come To Your Window

Words by Lorenzo da Ponte **Music by Wolfgang Amadeus Mozart**
from Don Giovanni

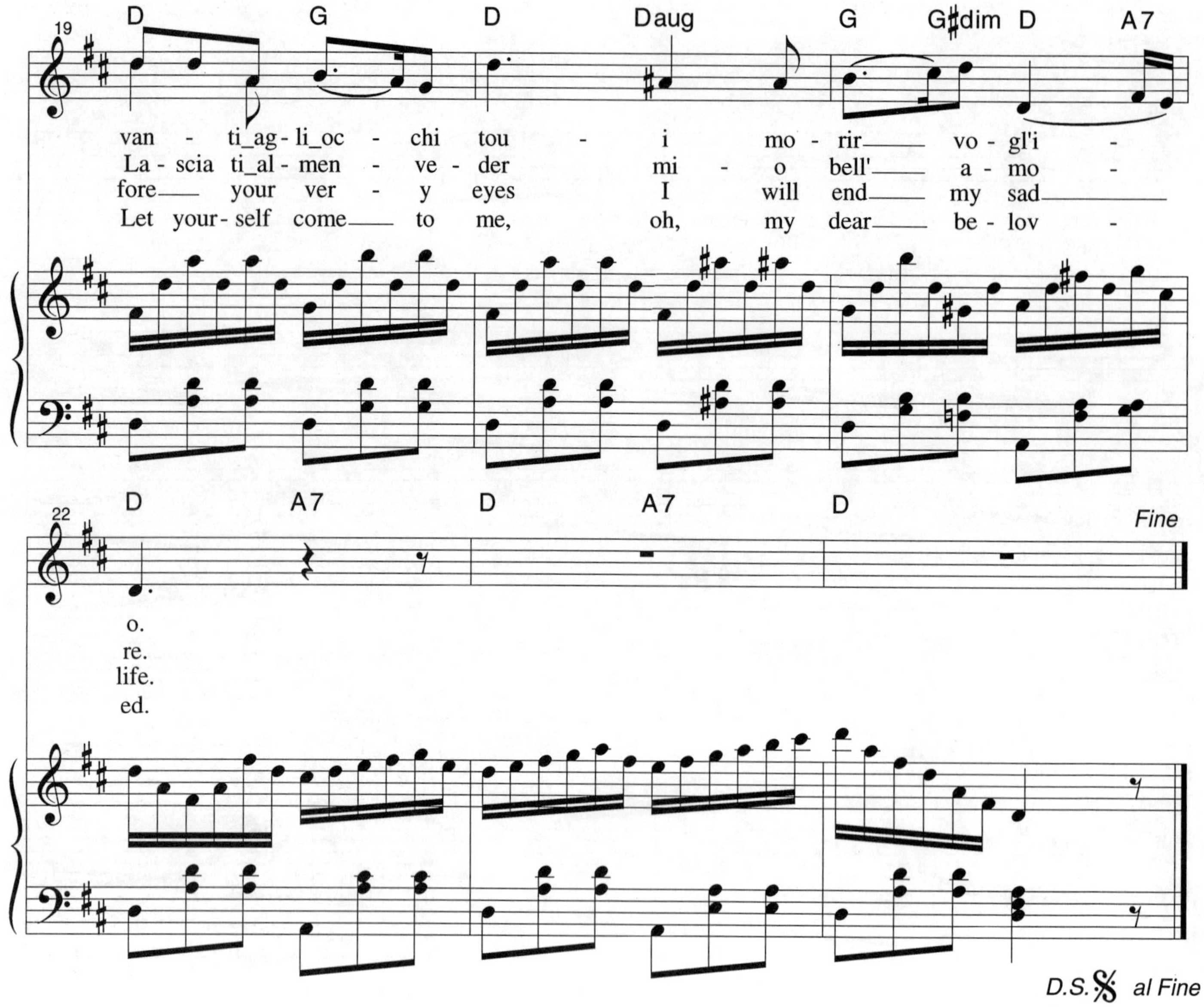
D G D Daug G G♯dim D A7
19
van - ti_ag - li_oc - chi tou - i mo - rir vo - gl'i -
La - scia ti_al - men - ve - der mi - o bell' a - mo -
fore your ver - y eyes I will end my sad
Let your - self come to me, oh, my dear be - lov -
D A7 D A7 D
22
Fine
o.
re.
life.
ed.
D.S. al Fine

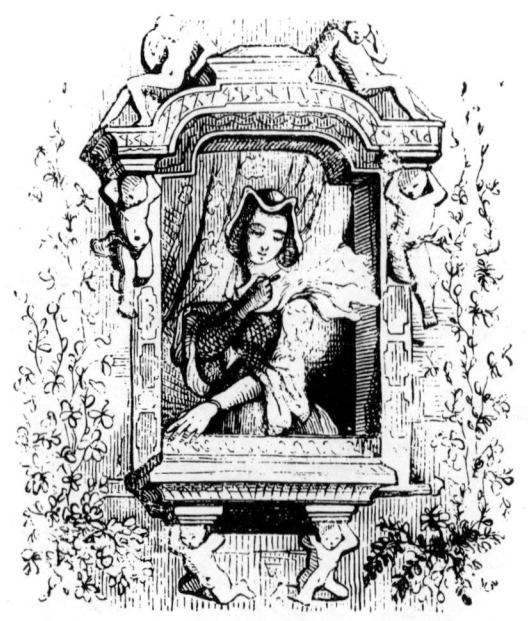

Una furtiva lagrima
A Furtive Tear

Words by Felice Romani **Music by Gaetano Donizetti**
from L'elisir d'amore

La donna è mobile
Woman Is Changeable

Words by Francesco Maria Piave **Music by Giuseppe Verdi**
from Rigoletto

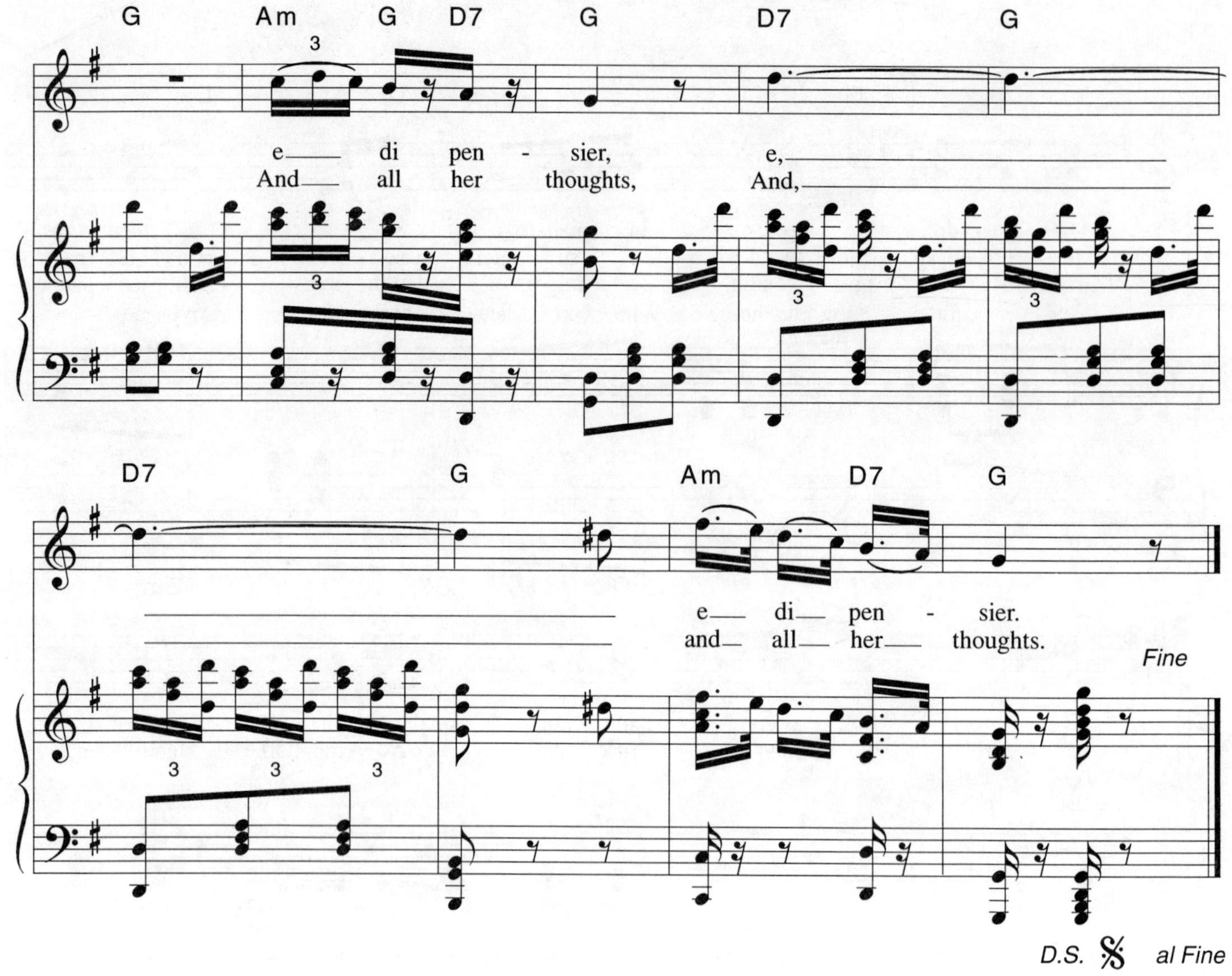
G Am G D7 G D7 G
e— di pen - sier, e,—
And— all her thoughts, And,—
D7 G Am D7 G
e— di— pen - sier.
and— all— her— thoughts.
Fine
D.S. al Fine

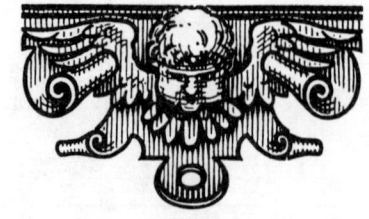

O Lola bianca
Oh, Lola, Fairest

Words by Giovanni Verga

Music by Pietro Mascagni
from Cavalleria Rusticana

M'appari tutt' amor
She Seemed To Me

Original German text
by Friedrich Wilhelm Riese

Music by Friedrich von Flotow
from Martha

Ah sì, ben mio
Ah Yes, My Love

Words by Salvatore Cammarano **Music by Giuseppe Verdi**
from Il Trovatore

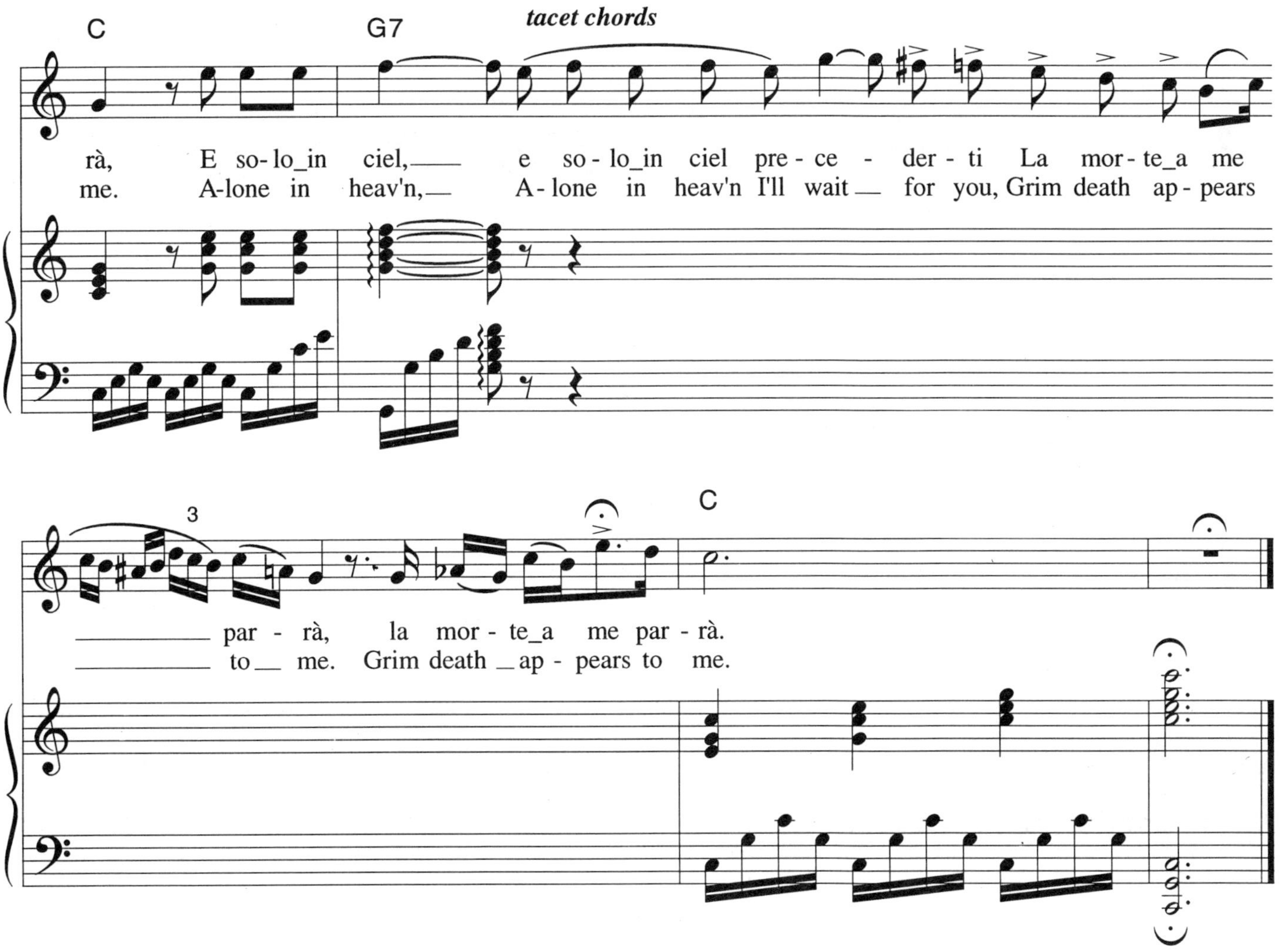
C
G7
tacet chords
rà, E so-lo_in ciel, e so-lo_in ciel pre-ce-der-ti La mor-te_a me
me. A-lone in heav'n, A-lone in heav'n I'll wait for you, Grim death ap-pears
3
C
par-rà, la mor-te_a me par-rà.
to me. Grim death ap-pears to me.

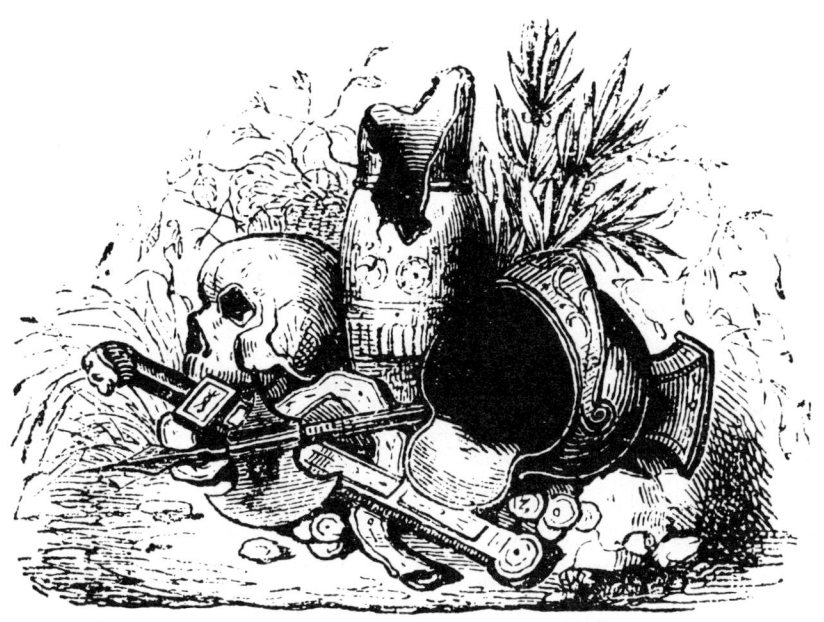

Vesti la giubba
Put On The Jacket

Words and Music by Ruggiero Leoncavallo
from Pagliacci